Who Lives in the Snow?

Jennifer Berry Jones

illustrated by Consie Powell

ROBERTS RINEHART

Lanham • New York • Boulder • Toronto • Plymouth, UK

For my family—J.B.J.
For Mom and Dad, with love—C.B.P.

Published by Roberts Rinehart Publishers
An imprint of The Rowman & Littlefield Publishing Group, Inc.
4501 Forbes Boulevard, Suite 200, Lanham, Maryland 20706
http://www.rowman.com

10 Thornbury Road, Plymouth PL6 7PP, United Kingdom

Distributed by National Book Network

Text copyright © 2001 by Jennifer Berry Jones
Illustrations copyright © 2001 by Consie Powell
First Roberts Rinehart paperback edition published in 2012

British Library Cataloguing in Publication Information Available

The Court Wayne Press hardback edition of this book was previously cataloged by the
Library of Congress as follows:

Jones, Jennifer Berry.
    Who lives in the snow? / Jennifer Berry Jones : illustrated by Consie Powell.
      p. cm.
    Includes bibliographical references (p.).
    Summary: Explores the world of mites, spiders, shrews, votes, chipmunks, foxes,
  and other animals that live in the snow in winter, describing their homes, habitats, and
  survival techniques.
    1. Animals—Wintering Juvenile literature. [1. Animals—Wintering. 2. Winter]
  I. Powell, Consie, ill. II. Title.

QL753.J65   1999
591.4'2—dc21   99–29335

ISBN 978-1-57098-444-0 (pbk : alk. paper)
ISBN 978-1-57098-445-7 (electronic)

♾™ The paper used in this publication meets the minimum requirements of American
National Standard for Information Sciences—Permanence of Paper for Printed Library
Materials, ANSI/NISO Z39.48-1992.

Printed in China

A cold wind sweeps in from the north, bringing winter to the meadow. The air is filled with swirling flakes that quickly cover rocks and blanket the dry grasses. After the storm has passed, spruce boughs sag under the weight of the season's first snow.

In the next several months, many more storms will affect the animals and plants of the meadow. Sometimes the snow will mean the difference between life or death during the winter.

Now the deep snow glitters in the early morning light. Nothing moves. But the meadow is very much alive on this brisk winter day.

Below the surface of the snow, in a dark and mysterious winter world, shrews are hunting. Voles are gathering food from their underground storehouses, and insects are moving stiffly in the cold.

What is this secret world? It's called the *subnivean* zone, meaning "under snow," from the Latin word *nivis*. When a mouse moves about on the ground under the snow, it is in the subnivean zone. And when a weasel burrows through soft snow above the ground, it is also within the subnivean zone.

The subnivean zone is the winter home of many plants, insects, spiders, and small mammals. They depend on the yearly snowfall to survive the cold months.

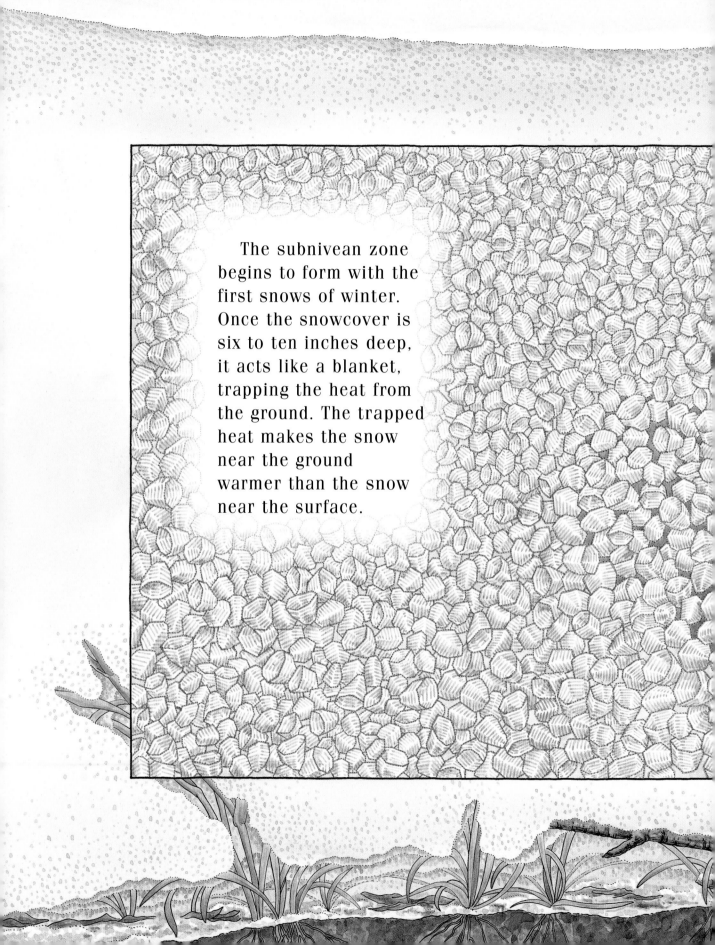

The subnivean zone begins to form with the first snows of winter. Once the snowcover is six to ten inches deep, it acts like a blanket, trapping the heat from the ground. The trapped heat makes the snow near the ground warmer than the snow near the surface.

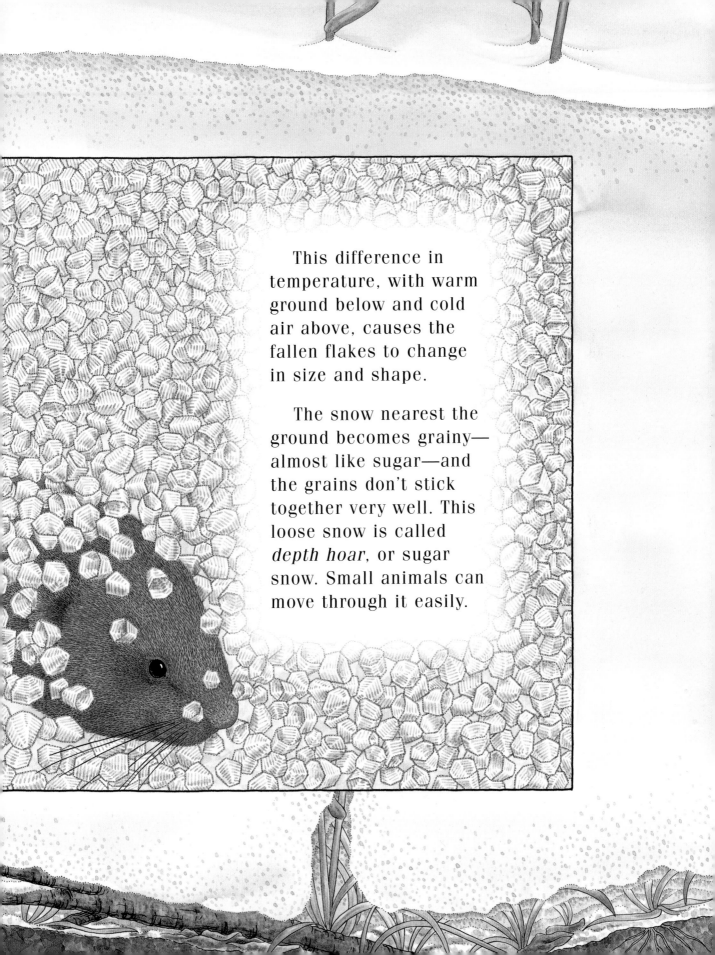

This difference in temperature, with warm ground below and cold air above, causes the fallen flakes to change in size and shape.

The snow nearest the ground becomes grainy—almost like sugar—and the grains don't stick together very well. This loose snow is called *depth hoar*, or sugar snow. Small animals can move through it easily.

By blocking winter winds, the *snowpack* provides a relatively warm living space for animals and plants. Many plants enter a *dormant*, or resting, stage during winter. But some plants, protected by the snow, are still green and actively growing. Certain seeds can actually sprout under six feet of snow! These under-snow plants are a vital food source for insects and small subnivean mammals.

ground beetle

larvae

Many kinds of insects die in the fall or become dormant in the winter. But a few insects are active all winter long, under and in the snow.

By digging deep into the soil, ground beetles and grubs—wormlike *larvae* that later grow into beetles—find protection from the cold. The beetles eat the *leaf litter*, which is made up of rotting leaves and bark on the ground. Other insects search for green plants.

Mites are very small creatures with four pairs
of legs, like spiders. Some kinds of mites thrive in
the cold, living in the leaf litter under the snow.
When it is unusually cold, they may not eat for
long periods.

mites

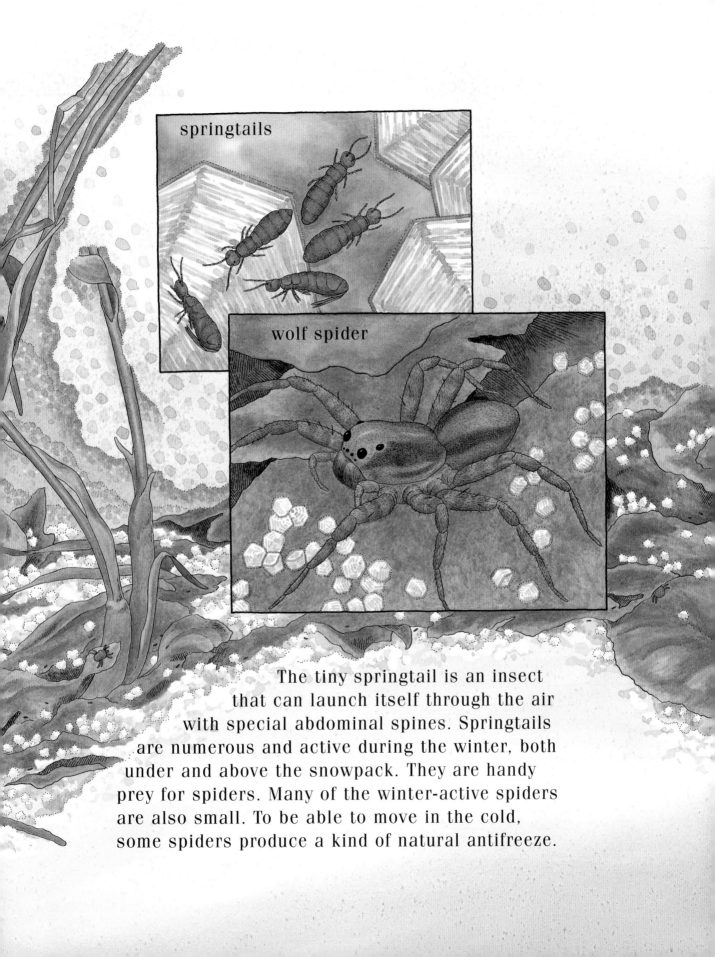

springtails

wolf spider

The tiny springtail is an insect
that can launch itself through the air
with special abdominal spines. Springtails
are numerous and active during the winter, both
under and above the snowpack. They are handy
prey for spiders. Many of the winter-active spiders
are also small. To be able to move in the cold,
some spiders produce a kind of natural antifreeze.

A constant danger for slow-moving spiders is the fearless, ever-hungry shrew. The shrew is an *insectivore*, feeding on insects and spiders.

One of the smallest mammals in the world, the shrew is also one of the most active, nearly always on the move. To have enough energy, it must eat often—at least its own body weight daily!

The shrew isn't sociable. Between frequent hunting trips, it rests alone in a well-insulated nest. To help keep warm, the animal depends on its special heat-producing brown fat.

The shrew's winter world is completely dark for several months, because the snow reflects most sunlight. In the darkness under the snow, the shrew's whiskers help it navigate along tunnels built by neighboring voles.

The vole, or meadow mouse, is a plant-eating *herbivore.* In the winter, some voles share a shallow underground nest, huddling with other voles. Small mammals sometimes pile together like this in cold weather to save body heat.

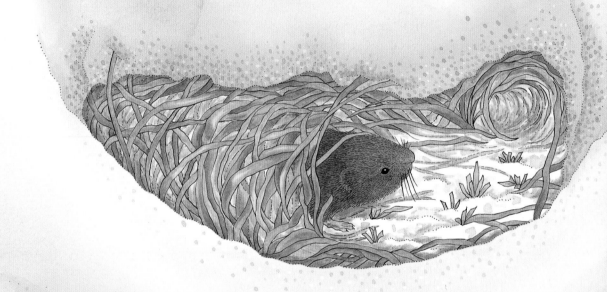

To reach its underground store of leaves and roots, the vole uses a network of tunnels it has built. Voles also use the clear spaces that are often found against logs or rocks under the snow.

Snow can actually flow like water, but very slowly. Sliding over a log like a snow waterfall, it flows straight down, leaving a tunnel against the log. Here small animals and insects can move freely.

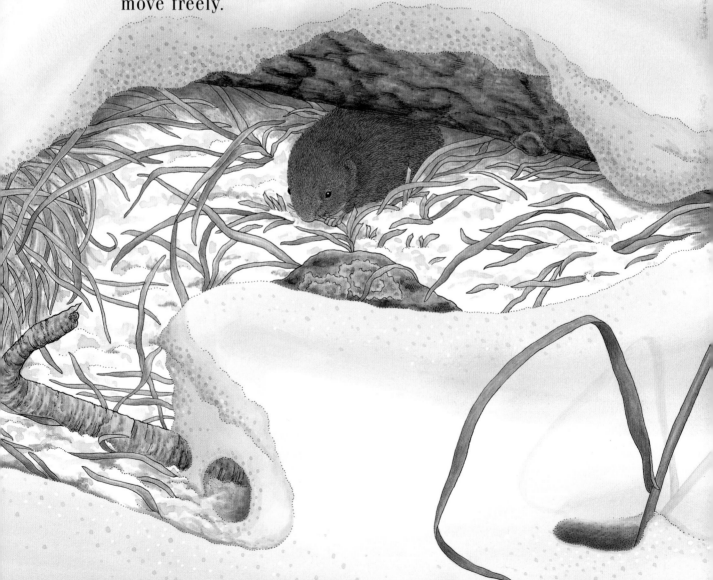

Sometimes voles burrow up through the snowpack, building tunnels clear to the surface. These may be air shafts, bringing in fresh air, or they may be "windows" to the winter world above the snow. We are still trying to learn just what the vole is doing.

Near the vole's nest, but deeper in the ground, a chipmunk is curled tight in its winter bed, *hibernating.* Several times during the winter, it will slowly awaken from this deep sleep to eat. The chipmunk will nibble on seeds that it stored under its mattress of leaves

Like its neighbor the vole, the chipmunk wants to see how winter is progressing. On warmer days, it may venture up through its tunnel to peek outside. And it may see danger at the edge of the meadow.

A red fox is looking for breakfast as she quietly surveys the meadow. To survive the winter, she hunts daily. The fox will eat whatever she can find, from insects to rabbits—and even dried berries left over from summer.

The alert fox moves softly. Suddenly she stops. Her keen ears have picked up faint sounds from deep under the snow.

Something small is rustling on the ground. Plunging nose-first into the soft snow, the fox snatches up a vole. She gobbles it down, but one vole isn't enough for a hungry fox on a cold day. She listens patiently. But there are no more voles here today, so the red fox moves on.

A small head pops up from the snow. Another *predator,* or hunter, is the long-tailed weasel. The tip of his tail is black all year round. In winter, the rest of his coat is snowy white, and in the summer his fur is brown. These color changes help the weasel to live without being seen by its enemies.

In winter, weasels hunt for small prey under the snow. The slender weasel burrows right through the snow and finds a mouse running along the ground.

Like the fox, the weasel hunts daily. The snow helps the weasel hide from enemies such as hawks. He lives wherever he finds a place, under a rock or log, or in another animal's old burrow.

Now two deer appear through the trees at the edge of the meadow. The deep snow keeps them from easily finding grasses or shrubs. Today they nibble on buds and tree bark. To reach the higher branches, they stretch up tall on their hind legs like slender ballerinas.

Many deer are in this area, all competing for the same food supply. If winter food runs low, some will die.

The winter months pass, and activity in the snow goes on. If alert predators like the fox and weasel don't disturb the residents below, midwinter is the best time for life in this hidden world.

In midwinter, the temperature under the snow
is relatively warm and stable. Nests are dry, and
as long as food supplies hold out, many animals
not only can survive but even produce young.

Gradually the days lengthen and begin to warm. Dim light filters through the melting snow. Scientists think that light coming through the snowpack may be a signal for plants to start growing.

Some early wildflowers, like snow buttercup and tansy mustard, sprout from seeds beneath the snowcover. Others like the glacier lily and spring beauty, begin to grow from fleshy roots and bulbs.

Strange as it seems, the warming days
of early spring can bring a new danger to
some subnivean animals. If a nest is built
where melting snow runs over it, the flood
can chill and drown small animals.

Finally, most of the snow is gone. Wildflowers
blow in the wind, and voles and shrews run
through fresh grass. Deer graze in the meadow,
and the red fox quickly finds breakfast.

But the time without snow is short. In only a few months, the snow will come again, silently filling the meadow. And deep under the icy cover, the secret winter world will return.

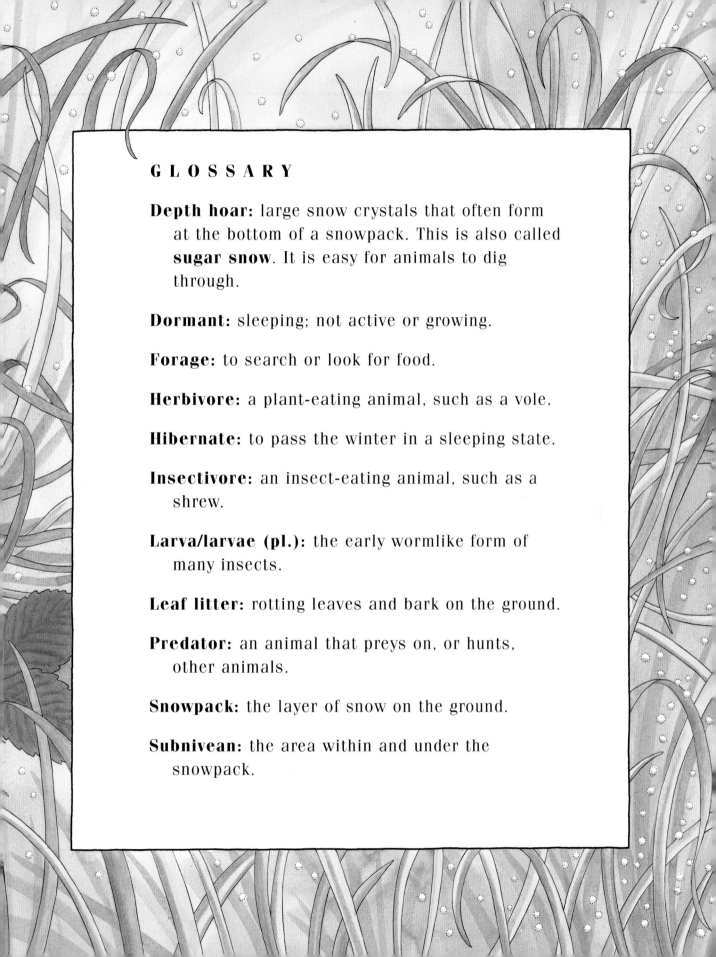

GLOSSARY

Depth hoar: large snow crystals that often form at the bottom of a snowpack. This is also called **sugar snow**. It is easy for animals to dig through.

Dormant: sleeping; not active or growing.

Forage: to search or look for food.

Herbivore: a plant-eating animal, such as a vole.

Hibernate: to pass the winter in a sleeping state.

Insectivore: an insect-eating animal, such as a shrew.

Larva/larvae (pl.): the early wormlike form of many insects.

Leaf litter: rotting leaves and bark on the ground.

Predator: an animal that preys on, or hunts, other animals.

Snowpack: the layer of snow on the ground.

Subnivean: the area within and under the snowpack.

SUGGESTED READING

To learn more about animals in winter and life in and under the snow, look for these books and magazine articles in your public library:

Bailey, Jill. *Discovering Shrews, Moles and Voles.* New York: Bookwright, 1989.

Fellman, Bruce. "When the Going Gets Cold," *National Wildlife*, Vol. 29:6 (Dec. 1990/Jan. 1991), pp. 10–12.

Fisher, Ron. *Animals in Winter.* Washington, D.C.: National Geographic Society, 1982.

Halfpenny, James C. "Cold Facts of Winter," *Natural History*, Vol. 100:12 (Dec. 91), pp. 52-60.

Halfpenny, James C. "Only the Tough Survive," *Ranger Rick*, Vol. 27:12 (Dec. 1993), p. 24–31.

Halfpenny, James C. and Roy Douglas Ozanne. *Winter: An Ecological Handbook.* Boulder, Colo.: Johnson Books, 1989.

Marchand, Peter J. "The Underside of Winter," *Natural History*, Vol. 102:2 (Feb. 1993), pp. 50–57.

Markle, Sandra. *Exploring Winter.* New York: Atheneum, 1984.

Ross, Drew. "Secrets Beneath the Snow," *Backpacker*, Vol. 25:156 (Feb. 1997), pp. 26–27.

ACKNOWLEDGMENTS

To the biologists and others who generously shared their knowledge with me, I owe many thanks. The comments of Cassie W. Aitchison, James K. Wangberg, Bruce Cutler, Tim Susman, Scott W. Gillihan, Roger A. Powell, Maureen Stanton, and Neil Souther were most helpful. I'm especially indebted to James Halfpenny for sharing his expertise of the winter world of Yellowstone National Park, and for his thoughtful suggestions. Special thanks go to Betsy Armstrong, snow scientist, and to my husband Wes.

—J.B.J.